P9-BYL-202

TO MOM
Merry
Christmas
1974
from
stacey

We Planted Miracles Today, Lord

# We Planted Miracles Today, Lord

## A Mother's Meditations and Prayers

By Barbara Burrow
Illustrated by Lilian Weytjens

Hallmark Editions

# We Planted
# Miracles Today, Lord

Lord,

I've been asking myself lately,

"Would You be at home in my home?"

It gives me a lot to work for.

I think it was the laughter
of our children
that prompted my husband
to touch my fingers and say,
"I love you."
We share a precious joy.

We planted flowers today, Lord.
My youngest kept calling them "miracles"
instead of marigolds. We laughed
and had a wonderful time together
planting your "miracles."

"Can we go to the park, Mommy?"
the children clamored early this morning.
My "maybe tomorrow" response brought
a loud protest from them.

"That's what you said yesterday,
and it's tomorrow now!"
Lord, help me to keep from putting
off until tomorrow those things
that should be done today.

Picking up toys and straightening
the patio, I had been oblivious
to the awesome beauty of the evening
until my husband joined me.
How much more meaningful
everything becomes
when shared with those we love.

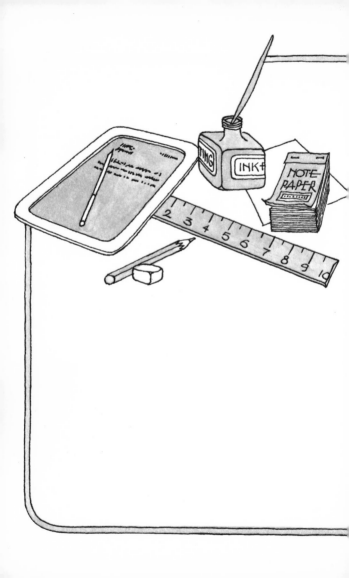

Report cards came out today.

I was so proud of the children.

I wonder how I would be graded, Lord,

in patience...in faith...in love?

I think I'd give myself

a great big "room for improvement."

We were only gone for the weekend,
but when we picked the children up
at their grandmother's house,
they clung to us like glue.
As I tucked our youngest
into his own bed,
he sighed, "Now we're whole again."

Lord, I think I'll put a sign
in the bedroom hall:

CAREFUL-
CHILDREN
GROWING

My youngest child called me outdoors
to see a family of baby rabbits.
I was late getting supper,
but I have come to realize
that growing children and animals
won't wait around
until you have time for them.

I was helping my sleepy son
with his prayer tonight.
"And help me to be good,"
I prompted him.
He added obediently,
"And help Mommy to be good."
Lord, please answer his prayer.

A neighbor quizzed my son:

"I understand you have a

little colored boy in your class."

His eyes lit up.

"Really?" he asked with interest.

"What color?"

The woman who lives two doors down

brought us a pie today. She said she

was making one for her family

and it was no trouble to make

another for us. I hope I am equally

as thoughtful of others.

My friend brought me a vial of perfume
for my birthday. I know it was her own,
and she hadn't the money
to buy me a gift.
Bless her for her unselfishness.
And thank You for the love
of friends like her.

I saw the "grouch" down the street today.

You know, the one who's always

calling the police on someone.

He was spraying his roses, and we had

the nicest talk about flowers.

You know, Lord,

I think he's just terribly lonely.

Help me to break

through the barriers

that lonely people erect

to keep from being hurt.

If I suddenly decided to lock myself
away from the world, would there be
an "empty spot"
where I had been?

It hurts to stand by
and watch people make mistakes, Lord,
especially those we love.
Help me to remember that I
cannot live their lives for them.
I can only give them my unqualified love.

We helped the Scouts plant
200 little fir trees today.
The children were tired and dirty,
but beaming with pride. They seem
to understand that much is expected
of them if they are to have
a beautiful green world
for their tomorrows.
O Lord, please let it be.

Today I felt the need to be by myself.
I was exhausted
from all the demands put upon me.
So I "skipped out" from everyone.
I needed it, but You know, Lord,
it felt good to get back
to those who need me.

Lord, I don't understand
my new neighbor at all.
Help me to love her.

Maybe it's because

I'm a woman...

and a mother...and a wife,

but I can't help believing

that peace is possible,

if only we can learn to love.

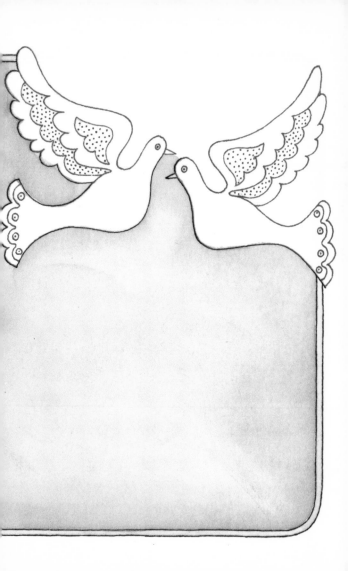

Today at the nursing home
one of the patients sharply told me,
"Don't bother me! I don't need anybody!"
My immediate response was one of anger.
I realize now that I judged him
too quickly. His hostile words were really
a plea for acceptance. Lord, help me
to see beneath the surface,
to "listen" with my heart.

Because my children kept telling me
how beautiful our new neighbor was,
I was surprised to meet a very
plain-looking woman. Then I watched
her beaming smile as she
passed out cookies and hugs
to the children,
and I thought, "They're right.
She IS beautiful!"

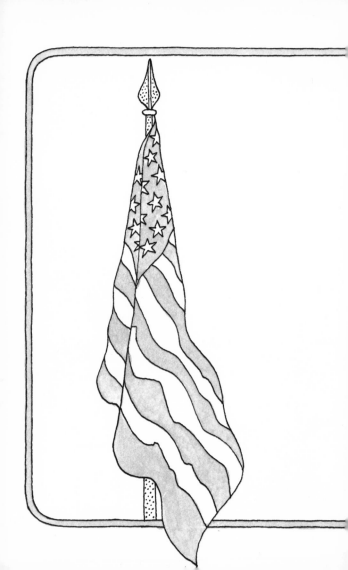

I went to a school assembly this morning.
When I heard those sweet young voices
singing "The Star-Spangled Banner,"
I almost cried. May they never lose
their pride in this glorious country
You have given us.

I love my quiet times, they are so few.
I let my mind drift and dream.
And though I may not speak
to You, Lord, I know
that You are very close to me
in those moments.